Destination Detectives

Kenya

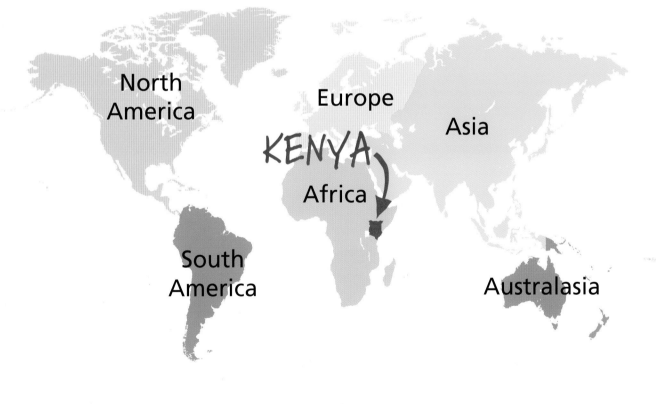

North
America

Europe

Asia

KENYA

Africa

South
America

Australasia

Rob Bowden

www.raintreepublishers.co.uk
Visit our website to find out more information about **Raintree** books.

To order:
☎ Phone 44 (0) 1865 888112
🗎 Send a fax to 44 (0) 1865 314091
💻 Visit the Raintree Bookshop at www.raintreepublishers.co.uk to browse our catalogue and order online.

Produced for Raintree by
White-Thomson Publishing Ltd,
Bridgewater Business Centre,
210 High Street, Lewes, BN7 2NH

First published in Great Britain by Raintree,
Halley Court, Jordan Hill, Oxford OX2 8EJ,
Part of Harcourt Education.
Raintree is a registered trademark of
Harcourt Education Ltd.

Editorial: Sonya Newland, Melanie Waldron,
and Lucy Beevor
Design: Gary Frost
Picture Research: Amy Sparks
Production: Chloe Bloom

Originated by Modern Age
Printed and bound in China
by South China Printing Company

10 digit ISBN 140620305X
13 digit ISBN 9781406203059
10 9 8 7 6 5 4 3 2 1
11 10 09 08 07 06

British Library Cataloguing in Publication Data
Bowden, Rob
    Kenya. - (Destination Detectives)
    1. Kenya - Geography - Juvenile literature 2. Kenya -
    Social life and customs - Juvenile literature 3. Kenya -
    Civilization - Juvenile literature
    I. Title
    967.6'2043

Acknowledgements
Jonathan Bonnick pp. 38-39; Rob Bowden pp. 5, 7t,
14, 26, 29, 31t, 31b, 33, 35, 38, 40, 41; Corbis pp. 9
(Adrian Arbib), 12 (Yann Arthus-Bertrand), 16 (Carl & Ann
Purcell), 19 (Wendy Stone), 27 (Gideon Mendel); 30 (David
Butow); Exile Images pp. 21 (H. Davies); Joanna Haskova
pp. 36; Marian Kaplan Photography pp. 8; Photolibrary
pp. 4 (Robert Harding Picture Library), 34 (David Cayless),
37 (Index Stock Imagery), 42 (Ariadne Van Zandbergen),
43 (David W. Breed); Popperfoto pp. 13; WTPix pp. 5t, 5m,
5b, 7b, 10, 11, 14-15, 17t, 17b, 18, 20-21, 22, 23, 24, 25,
28, 32, 39.

Cover photograph of Masai dance reproduced
with permission of Photolibrary/David Cayless

The paper used to print this book comes from
sustainable resources.

Contents

Where in the world? 4

A varied land 6

Clues from the past 8

From tip to toe 12

City life....................................18

Life in the countryside 24

Transport & travel 28

Food & culture............................32

Wildlife & tourism 36

Stay or go?................................42

Find out more..............................44

Kenya – facts & figures 46

Glossary....................................47

Index 48

Any words appearing in the text in bold, **like this,** are explained in the glossary. You can also look out for them in the Word Bank box at the bottom of each page.

Where in the world?

Majestic Masai

The Masai are Kenya's best-known **ethnic group**. They live in Kenya's Rift Valley and are **pastoralists** who live by herding cattle. The Masai live alongside Africa's wildlife. Many Masai now work as **safari** guides for tourists visiting Kenya's national parks.

You are awoken by a gentle flapping noise. You open your eyes to find yourself lying in bed inside a luxurious tent. Realizing it is not the tent that is flapping, you get up and peer outside into the bright dawn.

As your eyes adjust to the light, you can make out a large shape between the trees beyond your tent. The shape moves and there's that flapping noise again – it's an elephant flapping its ears as it walks along!

In parts of Kenya, the Masai still wear their traditional red dress and beaded jewellery.

WORD BANK   ethnic group people who share the same origins and culture
pastoralist someone who lives by caring for livestock

A Kenyan safari

You are just thinking about all the countries that might have elephants when a vehicle pulls up. As the driver climbs out of the vehicle, you notice a sign on the door: *Kenya Wildlife Service – Park Ranger*. At least you know where you are now! "Jambo – welcome to Kenya," says the ranger, "and welcome to the Masai Mara National Park." She invites you to join the other rangers for breakfast. What a fantastic opportunity to find out more about Kenya – and your tummy is rumbling too!

Every year, thousands of people go on safari to see elephants and other wildlife in the Masai Mara National Park.

Find out later...

Which lake do thousands of flamingos live on?

What are these women carrying in the baskets on their heads?

Which animals are Kenya's top tourist attraction?

A varied land

Over breakfast in the park offices, the rangers tell you all about their country, Kenya. A map on the wall has some notes left on it by the wardens and other visitors. These tell you about some of the different places in Kenya.

Kenya at a glance

SIZE:
582,646 square kilometres (224,961 square miles)

OFFICIAL NAME:
Republic of Kenya

POPULATION:
34 million

CAPITAL: Nairobi

GOVERNMENT:
Multiparty republic (run by several different political parties)

OFFICIAL LANGUAGES:
English and Kiswahili

CURRENCY:
Kenyan Shilling (Ksh)

The Rift Valley runs the length of Kenya. In places, it is over 1,000 metres (3,280 feet) deep and 100 kilometres (62 miles) wide. It has many lakes and several volcanoes.

The area around Naivasha has many farms producing flowers and vegetables for export to Europe.

Kisumu lies on the shores of Africa's largest lake, Lake Victoria. It is an important centre for the country's fishing industry.

Mount Kenya is Africa's second-highest mountain at 5,199 metres (17,057 feet).

Kenya's coastline stretches for 536 kilometres (333 miles) along the Indian Ocean. It has beautiful beaches and spectacular **coral reefs**.

WORD BANK coral reef long line of coral, close to the surface of the sea

Nairobi is the capital of Kenya, and the centre for the Government. It has a population of around 2.8 million people and is the biggest city in East Africa.

A rail town

Nairobi began life as a swamp used by the Masai to water their cattle. The British reached Nairobi in 1899. They were building a railway from Mombasa, on Kenya's coast, to neighbouring Uganda. Nairobi became a supply station and camp for the railway workers. It has since grown into one of Africa's biggest cities.

The area around Kericho is famous for its tea. Kenya is one of the world's biggest tea producers.

Clues from the past

The Leakey family

The Leakeys are a family of **paleontologists**. They have made many amazing discoveries of human ancestors in Kenya. Louis and Mary Leakey began this work in the 1930s. Their son Richard Leakey and his wife Meave, carried on their studies in the 1960s. In 1999, their daughter, Louise Leakey, joined the team to continue the family's incredible discoveries.

One of the rangers explains a bit about Kenya's history. It has one of the longest human histories of any country in the world. One of the best places to learn about this is the area around Lake Turkana, in the far north of the country.

Human ancestors

The oldest remains of human **ancestors** have been found in East Africa. These remains belong to a group called *hominids*, from which apes and humans evolved. In Kenya, some of the remains discovered around Lake Turkana and the Tugen Hills are up to six million years old! Another important site is Olorgesalie, around 60 kilometres (37 miles) to the south-east of the capital Nairobi. Here, stone axes and tools, as well as ancient body remains, have been found.

Richard Leakey holds up the skulls of human ancestors discovered in Kenya.

WORD BANK ancestor person you are descended from
hide skin of an animal

Early settlers

The people living around Lake Turkana belong to **ethnic groups** whose ancestors came from the Nile Valley around 2,500 years ago. Their way of life has changed very little since this time. They include the Turkana and Pokot peoples, who depend on their cattle and other livestock for survival. There are around 300,000 Turkana in north-western Kenya. They live in simple houses called *awi*. This part of Kenya is still cut off from the rest of the country, with no telephones or electricity, and only one large road.

A Turkana woman pours water for a herd of goats to drink, in a village in north-western Kenya.

The Turkana

The Turkana depend on cattle and other animals to survive. Cattle **hides** are used to make their huts, and for sleeping mats and sandals. Cattle also provide the traditional food of the Turkana – a nutritious drink made from cows' milk and blood.

paleontologist scientist who studies fossils to learn about the history of life on Earth

Outside contact

Traders from the **Arabian Peninsula** first arrived on the Kenyan coast around 1,100 years ago. By AD 1300 they had begun to settle around Mombasa and Malindi, trading ivory and slaves.

In 1498, the Portuguese explorer Vasco da Gama became the first European to reach Kenya. The Portuguese struggled with Arab peoples for control of the Kenyan coast. They fought many battles over the valuable trade to be found there. By the end of the 16th century, the Portuguese controlled much of the coast, including Mombasa.

Mau Mau

The Mau Mau was a secret group of tribesmen in Kenya, who tried to drive the British out of the country. The group was formed in 1944 and began to attack British settlers in 1952. This resulted in a war between the Mau Mau and the British. By 1956, when the Mau Mau were defeated, more than 13,000 people had been killed in the rebellion.

Fort Jesus was built by the Portuguese in 1593 to guard the port at Mombasa from attacks by the Arabs.
➤

Arabian Peninsula area between Africa and Asia that includes countries like Saudi Arabia

Colonial rule

In 1890, the United Kingdom claimed control of Kenya, and ruled the country for 73 years. The British influence can still be seen all over Kenya, from the education system to the architecture, in old buildings like the Norfolk Hotel in Nairobi. The British also started many of Kenya's industries, such as the tea and coffee industries, and even tourism with the early **safaris**.

Independence

Kenya gained independence from the United Kingdom on 12 December 1963. Since then it has become one of the most important countries in Africa. Many international companies have their African bases in the capital Nairobi, and so does the **United Nations**. Kenya has also become one of Africa's leading tourist destinations.

Kenya's presidents

Kenya has had only three presidents since it gained its independence from the United Kingdom in 1963. Jomo Kenyatta became the country's first president, and was in power until he died in 1978. Daniel Toroitich Arap Moi became the next president until 2002, when President Mwai Kabaki came to power.

The parliament building in Nairobi was built in 1952, when the country was under British rule.

United Nations (UN) global development organization that most countries belong to

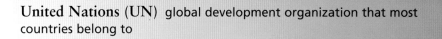

From tip to toe

In the morning, you decide to leave Lake Turkana and make the three-day journey to Mombasa, on the southern coast of Kenya. This will be a great chance to discover Kenya's many different environments.

Heat and dust

As you head south along the floor of the Rift Valley, the land is dry and dusty, with occasional plants. To the east lie the Chalbi desert and the dry plains of northern Kenya. Few people live in these lands because it is so difficult to grow food or find water, but you see some **pastoralists** with their camels and cattle.

The Jade Sea

Lake Turkana is the largest permanent desert lake in the world. The lake covers an area of around 6,475 square kilometres (2,500 square miles). Temperatures in this area can reach 33°C (91°F). Lake Turkana is sometimes called the Jade Sea because the **algae** living there turn its water a deep green.

A volcano stands next to the green waters of Lake Turkana in north-west Kenya.

➤

WORD BANK   algae small plant, similar to seaweed
altitude the distance above sea level used to measure height

The temperature outside is over 30°C (86°F), but it can get much hotter than that, especially before the rains. Kenya has two rainy seasons. The long rains fall between March and May, and there is a shorter rainy season throughout October and November.

Cool and green

A few hours later the surroundings have changed. The land is greener, with trees and small fields growing vegetables. You are now climbing out of the valley floor and on to one of the **escarpments** that form the edges of the Rift Valley. You notice that it is much cooler. This is because you are at a higher **altitude** now. Mount Kenya is the highest point in the country, at 5,199 metres (17,057 feet). It is so cold at this altitude that there is snow on top of the mountain!

Running on high

Kenya's runners are some of the best in the world. Nearly all of them come from just a few tribal groups living in the highlands of the Rift Valley. Living at high altitude is known to make you fitter. This might be one reason why Kenyan athletes are so successful.

Kenyan athlete Christopher Koskei wins the gold medal for the 3,000 metres at the World Athletics Championships in 1999.

Power from below

The area south of Lake Naivasha has lots of volcanic activity. The underground heat here is used to generate electricity. Superheated steam is taken from the ground and used to drive turbines in **geothermal** power stations at Olkaria. This energy provides around 10 percent of Kenya's electricity.

At the Olkaria geothermal power station, steam from deep under the ground is used to create electricity.

Western highlands

From the rim of the Rift Valley, your route continues towards Nairobi through the western highlands. This region has good soil, warm temperatures, and year-round sun. It also has regular rainfall. These conditions make the western highlands perfect for farming. The towns of Eldoret, Kitale, and Nakuru are important farming centres in this region. Most British people settled here during colonial times. The area was once known as the "white highlands" because of all the white people that lived there.

Many of the crops grown here are for local use, including maize, potatoes, tomatoes, carrots, cabbage, and onions. Others are grown for **export**, including coffee and sugar. There are many large **plantations** growing these crops.

WORD BANK   diatom small algae-like plant with a shell
geothermal energy produced by natural heat

Around Kericho, the land is carpeted with neat green tea bushes. Kericho is one of the world's biggest tea-producing regions, and most people living here work in the fields or factories of the big tea estates.

Salt lakes

To the east of Kericho, the road begins to fall again into the Rift Valley and towards Nakuru. Nakuru is famous for its lake. The water entering the lake has nowhere to go – there are no rivers flowing out of it towards the sea. This means that as its water evaporates, it leaves behind minerals that make the water very salty. In these conditions, blue-green **algae** and **diatoms** thrive, and attract flamingos who feed on them.

Kenyan tea

In 2004, Kenya was the world's biggest exporter of tea, exporting 293,000 tonnes (288,371 tons) of the 328,000 tonnes (322,818 tons) produced in the country.

A royal lake

Lake Victoria is Africa's largest lake, and the third largest (in surface area) in the world. It was named after the British queen of the time by the British explorer John Hanning Speke. Speke was the first European to reach the lake, in July 1858.

Sometimes there can be as many as one million flamingos on Lake Nakuru at one time!

plantation large farm growing a single crop

The highlands

You reach Nairobi, located on the eastern edge of the Rift Valley. You are now at an **altitude** of around 1,700 metres (5,577 feet). At this altitude the **climate** is pleasant, with average day temperatures of around 24°C (75°F). At night it can feel cold, however, and temperatures can drop as low as 5°C (41°F).

Savannah lands

Leaving Nairobi on the road to Mombasa, the landscape around you is made up of grassland dotted with trees. This is Kenya's **savannah** land, which covers large areas of southern Kenya. The grasslands provide pasture for the cattle of the Masai people, and are also home to most of Kenya's spectacular wildlife. Some savannah is protected by national parks, and the road you are on passes right though Kenya's largest – Tsavo National Park.

A herd of wildebeest gather at a watering hole in the Tsavo National Park.

Fast fact

As you climb higher, the temperature drops by about 0.6°C for every 100 metres in altitude, or 3.5°F for every 1,000 feet. This is called the "lapse rate".

WORD BANK   Equator imaginary line round the middle of Earth
hydroelectric power generated by moving water

Coastal Kenya

At sea level in Mombasa the climate is hotter and humid. Mombasa is a busy city, but to the north and south there are beautiful white-sand beaches, which are popular with tourists. **Mangrove forests** and **coral reefs** are found along the coast here. These provide a **habitat** for important marine wildlife. Just offshore lie several small islands. The best-known of these is Lamu, in the north.

Survival tip

The **Equator** runs right through Kenya, which means that the sun is extra powerful here. Make sure you wear sunscreen to protect your skin.

The white-sand beaches and warm weather attract thousands of tourists to Mombasa every year.

Men stack logs from the mangrove forests on the island of Lamu.

Rivers

Kenya's rivers are quite small, and flow into the country's lakes or the Indian Ocean. The Tana and Galana rivers are the longest in Kenya. They flow from the highlands east of Nairobi to the Indian Ocean. The Tana river has many dams built across it to generate **hydroelectric** power (HEP). Around two-thirds of Kenya's electricity comes from HEP.

mangrove forest type of tropical forest that grows in shallow coastal waters
savannah tropical grassland, often dotted with trees

City life

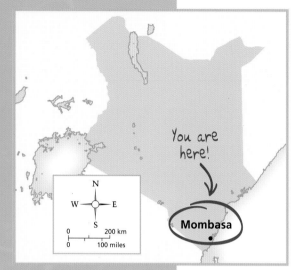

You are here!

Mombasa

You have finally reached your destination of Mombasa. Everywhere you look there are people, and it is quite a shock after three days of huge, open spaces. You start to wonder about all these people. How many are there? Where are they from? How do they live? As you think about these questions you notice a large school building. Inside, on the wall, there is a big display about the people of Kenya.

Mombasa is the second-largest city in Kenya, with a population of around 900,000. It is an important port.

Unevenly spread

Kenya's population is not evenly spread across the country. The highest **population density** is in Nairobi, where there are more than 3,150 people per square kilometre (8,100 per square mile). In the north-east of the country, there are only 8 people per square kilometre (20 per square mile).

WORD BANK population density number of people living in a certain area
rural relating to the countryside

The people of Kenya

- Kenya's population was nearly 34 million in 2005.
- The population is increasing by about 2.3 percent every year.
- By 2030, Kenya will have over 41 million people.
- Where people live: **Urban** areas – 42 percent. **Rural** areas – 58 percent.
- Kenya's biggest cities are Nairobi, Mombasa, Nakuru, Kisumu, and Eldoret.
- The average Kenyan woman will have four children.
- Kenyans born today can expect to live for an average of 46 years, due to the effect of the **AIDS epidemic**.
- Kenya's main **ethnic groups**: Kikuyu – 22 percent; Luhya – 14 percent; Luo – 13 percent; Kalenjin – 12 percent; Kamba – 11 percent; other – 28 percent.

You decide that it is important to find out more about what life is like for people living in Kenya today. The best place to do this is in Nairobi – Kenya's capital and its biggest city, so you head off to catch a train there.

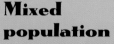

Mixed population

Most people in Kenya are Black Africans, but Kenya is also home to people who are originally from the **Arabian Peninsula**, Asia, and Europe. Kenya has around 40,000 Arabic people, 40,000 Europeans, and 80,000 Asians (mainly Indians). These people first came to Kenya because of trade or during the colonial period. Many of the younger generation were born in Kenya and consider it their home.

Many black Kenyans are highly educated and work in specialized industries.

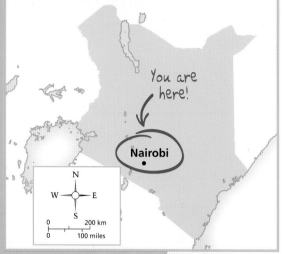

You are here!

Nairobi

N
W — E
S

0   200 km
0   100 miles

Bustling Nairobi

From the train station in Nairobi, you head to the Kenyatta Conference Centre in the middle of the city. From the top you have a bird's-eye view of Nairobi. You can see tall office buildings, green parks, and busy roads crammed with vehicles. The city centre is the central business district (CBD), but there are no houses there. The people of the city live around the edges.

Slum life

Nairobi has some of the largest and most crowded slums anywhere in the world. At least 60 percent of the city's population live in the slums, and their population is growing by over 5 percent a year.

Tall, modern office blocks dominate the skyline of Nairobi's city centre.

Poverty and hope

Not far out of the city, you reach an enormous valley full of buildings. They are made of wood, metal, plastic, or anything else that is available. This is Mathare Valley, one of Nairobi's biggest **slums**. People come to the city to look for a better life, but many of them end up here in the slums. They are poor and cannot afford anything better. There is no piped water or electricity, and only a few shared toilets.

As you look around you, daily life carries on. There are shops selling groceries, a hairdressers, a second-hand clothes market, a school, and some children playing football. The children tell you they are part of a project called Mathare Youth Sports **Association**.

Thousands of people live in slums like this one on the outskirts of Nairobi.

Out of Africa

Not everyone in Kenya is poor. Some people lead very good lives in luxurious homes with swimming pools, gardens, and house staff. In Nairobi, the houses of the rich are clustered into wealthy areas of the city such as Karen and the Ngong Hills.

slum area of poor-quality housing

Improving life in the slums

To find out more about life in the **slums**, you talk to some of the children playing football. One of the boys tells you that although life can be difficult, people are working hard to improve things. He takes you to see some of the work being done.

The Mathare Youth Sports **Association** (MYSA) was set up in 1987. It began as a football club for young boys and girls living in the Mathare slum. The children are organized into teams and leagues, and play regular matches. Each team must also do things to improve their slum, and they are awarded points for doing this. Every Saturday, MYSA teams borrow tools and wheelbarrows to do environmental clean ups. This can include unblocking drains and clearing away piles of rubbish. Their work is making Mathare a cleaner and safer place to live, and is setting a good example for others to follow.

World famous

In 1992, the Mathare Youth Sports Association was awarded a global prize by the **United Nations** for its work towards improving the environment. In 2003 the MYSA was also a **nominee** for the Nobel Peace Prize. These have made the MYSA world famous.

A group of boys play near one of the slum settlements on the edge of the city.

People are working together in other slums, too. There are projects to build community schools, savings clubs to help people start businesses, and health centres for those with health problems.

As you say goodbye to the children at Mathare, you remember that over half of Kenya's people (58 percent) still live in **rural** areas, so that is the next place to investigate.

Projects like MYSA mean that children like these now have a chance of a better quality of life.

Keep it clean

The number of children under five years old who die in Nairobi's slums is two-and-a-half times higher than the number who die in Nairobi as a whole. Many of these deaths are because of the dirty environment. Projects such as MYSA can help to reduce these deaths.

Life in the countryside

On the move

Nomadic pastoralists can be found in many parts of northern Kenya. Local markets are important for pastoralists. They can buy and sell animals, and catch up on news from other pastoralists they meet there. Travelling vets visit the markets to look after the pastoralists' animals.

You head north of Nairobi and as soon as you leave the city you see fewer houses and more fields. Along the side of the road are stalls selling baskets of vegetables and fruit, and sacks of charcoal. Lorries sometimes stop and load up with these goods to take them into the city.

Rural life

The **rural** towns and villages you see are much smaller than the cities. Many don't have proper roads, just bumpy earth tracks. As vehicles go past, clouds of dust fill the air, but in the rainy season these tracks can turn into rivers of mud. You notice people digging in the fields. Others collect water on bicycles or balanced on their heads. At road junctions, there is nearly always a small market. People are busy selling things from their farms or buying **provisions** to take home. Some people are waiting for a lift and squeezing on to overcrowded buses, trucks, and cars.

Women carry goods in baskets on their heads along the side of a road in rural Kenya.
➤

WORD BANK nomadic people who move around rather than settling in one place
provisions supplies of food and other household items

Meeting place

You stop at a market, and the first thing you notice is that everyone is talking to one another. The market is not just for buying and selling. It is also where people meet to see friends, to share stories, and catch up on news. It is the centre of rural life.

Survival tip

Things in markets hardly ever have a fixed price. If you see something you like, you will have to bargain with the seller until you agree on a price.

End of the road

One of the most popular stalls in any rural market is the sandal stall. Old car tyres are **recycled** to make tough rubber sandals. Some people may walk over 10 kilometres (6 miles) a day, so a strong pair of sandals is an important possession!

Most villages in the Kenyan countryside have their own markets, where people gather to buy and sell all sorts of goods.

recycled used again for the same or a different use

Healthcare

In the corner of the market, people crowd around a lady with piles of dried leaves, seeds, berries, and bark. She is a local healer, and these are her medicines. Local healers often provide traditional medicine in **rural** areas because there are not many **clinics** or hospitals.

By world standards, healthcare in Kenya is poor, but this also depends where you live. In a city like Nairobi, there are good hospitals and clinics for those who can afford them. In rural areas, people may have to travel long distances on foot just to see a nurse or doctor. Kenya also suffers from a shortage of doctors, nurses, and drugs for treating people.

Know your plants

Local **healers** use plants for traditional medicines, but many normal Kenyans also have a good knowledge of the plants around them. In West Pokot, for example, small sticks of the Ashionion bush are used to make toothbrushes. The sap from the Tumwon bush is used to poison arrow-tips before hunting.

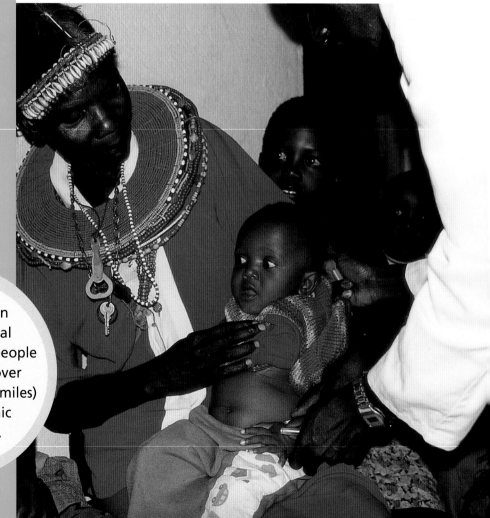

Healthcare can be poor in rural areas, and some people have to travel over 50 kilometres (30 miles) to reach a clinic like this one.

clinic local centre for providing basic healthcare

Education

Primary education in Kenya is provided free by the Government. However, parents have to buy uniforms, books, and stationery. They also have to pay for school lunches. Some children do not go to school at all because their parents cannot afford these things. Secondary schooling is not free, so many children leave school when they are quite young.

University education

Children who grow up in the **slums** or rural areas often have a poor education. However, children from wealthier families may go on to university. Kenya's main university is the University of Nairobi, in the capital city. It first opened in 1956, and now has over 22,000 students.

Survival tip

Drink plenty of water as you explore Kenya, but make sure it is bottled – not all water in Kenya is clean.

Although some rural schools can be basic, others have good facilities. This one near Kisumu helps children get a good education.

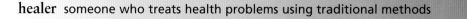

healer someone who treats health problems using traditional methods

Transport & travel

One thing you have noticed about Kenya is how many people walk places. They walk to market, to the doctors, to and from school, to the fields, and with their animals. It makes you think about how people in Kenya travel and what types of transport they have.

The long walk

Walking is the most common way of getting around in Kenya. This is because most people cannot afford other types of transport. Many people, especially the women, carry large items such as water cans, sacks of food, or bundles of wood with them. Most amazingly though, they carry them on their heads! This is called "headloading", and you have to have very good balance to make sure the items don't fall off!

Travelling farm

In **rural** areas of Kenya, pick-up trucks are used to transport people and goods over long distances. This can be an interesting experience and you might find yourself sitting on bags of maize, amongst pineapples, or potatoes. There may even be chickens and goats along for the ride. Anything goes, as long as it can squeeze in!

Children walk along the side of the road, with toys they have made themselves.

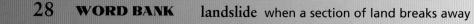

WORD BANK   landslide when a section of land breaks away

Animal power

Donkeys are used in many parts of Kenya to transport goods and people. They are especially useful in mountain regions, as they are good at climbing steep mountain tracks. Cattle are also used in some parts of the country to plough fields ready for planting, although tractors are now more common.

Fast fact
In Lamu, most of the roads are so narrow and winding that cars cannot get through, so donkeys are the method of transportation used there!

Gone in a flash

During the rainy season, many roads and tracks become difficult to use. In sudden downpours there can even be flash floods that cause **landslides** or wash away bridges. This can leave vehicles stranded for several days before help arrives.

A train of donkeys on a mountain track in the Cherangani Hills of the Rift Valley.

Boda bodas

Boda bodas are bicycle taxis, with the seat for the passenger on the back above the rear wheel. They are a cheap method of transport and are popular in many places. They were once used to transport people across border points between Kenya and Uganda, from border to border. That is how they got their name.

City travel

You decide to leave the countryside and head back to the cities to discover what other types of transport are used in Kenya. You catch a brightly painted bus with the word "Express" written on it. It is heading towards the city of Eldoret. As you get closer, the roads become busier with lorries carrying cargo, more buses, and many more cars. You cross a railway line and there is also a sign to an airport. With so many types of transport, Eldoret must be an important place.

Transport system

Kenya has several main transport hubs. These are important towns and cities where the many different types of transport come together – such as road, rail, and air. The main hubs in Kenya are Nairobi, Mombasa, Kisumu, Eldoret, and Nakuru. The road and rail network connects these hubs and picks up traffic from the places in between.

Nairobi is Kenya's most important transport hub. The streets are crowded with cars and trucks, as people make their way in and out of the city.

Local travel

From each transport hub, local transport services connect to nearby villages and smaller towns. Buses and shared taxis also travel on longer-distance routes to remote regions, and set off as soon as the vehicle is full. Within towns and cities the *matatu* is the most common type of public transportation. These are small minibuses that hold around twelve passengers. Most are white, but in Nairobi some are brightly painted. Nairobi's *matatus* are also well-known for playing very loud pop music, as a way of attracting more customers!

These brightly coloured motorized rickshaws are known as *tuk-tuks*, and are used as taxis.

Today, Kenya's railways are mainly used for transporting cargo goods.

End of the line?

The railway was responsible for opening up Kenya to the outside world, and was once an important trade route. Today, much of the 2,778 kilometres (1,700 miles) of railway is in poor condition, and there are very few services.

Food & culture

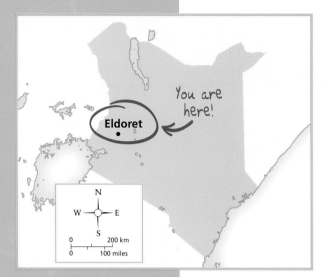

Eldoret
You are here!

N
W E
S

0   200 km
0   100 miles

The journey to Eldoret has made you hungry, so you set off to discover what foods Kenya has to offer. There is a wide variety of food available – from Western pizzas and burgers to Indian food. There are many local dishes too, but you might need some advice on what they are.

All sorts of fruit, vegetables and other food, like these different beans, can be bought fresh at market places in towns and villages.

Meat feast

Kenyans enjoy eating meat, particularly on special occasions. In Nairobi, a restaurant called Carnivore provides the ultimate meat feast. It even gives you the chance to try zebra, giraffe, impala, crocodile, ostrich, and other local game, all taken from special game farms.

Karibuni Diner Menu

MEAT AND FISH DISHES

NYAMA CHOMA – roasted meat (can be goat, mutton, or beef)

KUKU CHOMA – roasted chicken

MUSHKAKI – small pieces of meat cooked on **skewers** (like kebabs)

TILAPIA – a meaty white fish from Lake Victoria, grilled whole

MBUTA (NILE PERCH) – a large fish from Lake Victoria, served as fillets

VEGETABLE DISHES

IRIO – potato, cabbage, and beans mashed together

SUKUMA WIKI – boiled green leaves, normally of kale

UGALI – ground maize boiled with water (sometimes milk) into a solid paste

MATOKE – mashed **plantain**

MBOGA – potatoes, carrots, and onions (sometimes other vegetables) in a meaty gravy

SNACKS

MKATE MAYAI – thin pancake bread wrapped around a fried egg and minced meat

MANDAZI – deep fried sweet dough (similar to a doughnut)

FRUITS

MAEMBE – mango

MACHUNGWA – oranges

NANASI – pineapple

NDIZI – banana

PAPAI – paw paw/papaya

PERA – guava

DRINKS

MAZIWALALA – fermented milk

CHAI – tea

KAHAWA – coffee

Nyama choma

No matter where you go in Kenya, you will nearly always find a nyama choma restaurant. These sell just grilled meat, often with ugali. Nyama choma is popular for lunches and evening meals. With music and drinks many nyama choma restaurants also make for a great night out!

Maize is ground down in a maize mill. It will be boiled up with water to make ugali – a popular Kenyan dish.

skewer metal or wooden rod with a sharp end for holding meat whilst cooking

Beads

Beads have traditionally been used by Kenyans for making jewellery or for decorating hair. Kazuri Beads is a women's **cooperative** that continues these traditions by making modern bead necklaces and bracelets. Their beautiful beads are mainly for sale to tourists or for **export** to Europe and beyond. You can even buy them on the Internet!

Dancing and drumming

Many of the restaurants you pass are playing a loud mix of Western and local pop music. This can be heard all over Kenya now, and has replaced many traditional forms of music. Many other cultural traditions such as dance and fashion have also been replaced, but some customs remain.

The Masai and Samburu people are famous for their rhythmic leaping dance, in which they jump effortlessly into the air whilst chanting and singing. The dance is performed by men and has become a popular tourist attraction in many hotels and **safari** lodges. Some dancing is accompanied by drumming, another famous tradition for which the Mijikenda and Akamba people are well known.

Masais demonstrate their traditional jumping dance.
➤

clan group of families related through marriage

Fashion

Many people in Kenya wear Western fashions, but traditional clothing such as the *kanga* and *kikoi* are still quite common, especially among the people who live in the coastal regions.

The *kanga* is worn by women, and is a cotton wrap that is normally brightly coloured. The *kikoi* is a wrap worn by men around their lower body. It is less common, but still worn in **rural** areas and by older generations. The Masai are well-known for their bright red *kikois*.

Women of the Pokot people of eastern Kenya wear elaborate bead necklaces.

cooperative group of people working together

Wildlife & tourism

Safari tour

A typical 10-day Kenyan safari tour will include game drives in two or three national parks, luxury accommodation, and a visit to a Masai village. There will also be a chance for shopping in the Nairobi craft market and several days to relax on a Mombasa beach. Transport and a guide are also included.

All across Kenya, you can see arts and crafts for sale in small shops, or even just by the side of the road. Sometimes there are tourist minibuses and crowds of people looking for a souvenir to take home. Tourism must be an important industry, and you head to the tourist office in Eldoret to find out more.

On tour

Most tourists come to Kenya for its world-famous wildlife, but the lady in the tourist office explains that there are many other attractions in Kenya. There are mountains to climb, villages to visit, towns to explore, and the beautiful beaches and islands of the coast. She gives you a leaflet about tourism in Kenya, with some ideas about where to visit.

In some parts of Kenya, there are large workshops, where people sit and make items out of wood and other materials, which are sold as souvenirs to tourists.

Call of the wild

Kenya has the world's largest number of mammals in any one place. It provides a unique experience in a beautiful setting, and it is this that tourists come to see. It is so important that you decide to see for yourself! The tourist office helps organize a trip with a **safari** tour just about to leave for Amboseli National Park.

Tourism facts

- Kenya had nearly one million visitors in 2004.
- Earnings from tourism were £197 million in 2004.
- Tourism provides most of Kenya's foreign income.
- At least 500,000 people work in the tourist industry.
- Tourism can help preserve traditional cultures.

The main national parks and nature reserves in Kenya.

Safari tours will take you out in jeeps to see Kenya's wildlife in its natural environment.

Trekking

Kenya's mountains provide some great trekking opportunities. There are several routes to the top of Mount Kenya, and a trek will take at least four days. Mount Elgon is less steep and takes about three days. The Cherangani Hills in the Rift Valley are also excellent for trekking, and some treks can be done in a day.

Hunting the "Big Five"

In the days when Kenya was popular with **safari** hunters, five animals were the most prized treasures. They were the elephant, rhino, lion, leopard, and buffalo, and became known as the "Big Five". They are still hunted today, but with tourists' cameras instead of guns.

Members of an ecotourist operation unload a truck at Marich Pass, near Eldoret.

▼

People and wildlife

Amboseli National Park is one of Kenya's top tourist attractions. It is best known for the large elephant herds that roam the swamps and grasslands beneath Mount Kilimanjaro – Africa's highest mountain – which lies just across the Kenyan border in neighbouring Tanzania.

The Masai have grazed their cattle on the lands of Amboseli for hundreds of years, but in 1970 parts of the area were set aside for wildlife only. The Masai were angry at the loss of their lands and began killing many of the wild animals in protest. The Government gave them some of their land back and the Masai now live peacefully again.

Survival tip
Remember that wildlife can be dangerous. Always listen to your guides and keep quiet, even if you are excited!

ecotourism tourism that benefits local people and does not harm the environment

Valuing wildlife

People and wildlife compete for land elsewhere in Kenya, too. People are clearing more and more land for housing or farmland, and so wildlife is sometimes forced into areas where people live. Elephants are known for destroying entire harvests if they stray on to farmland, and lions and leopards occasionally kill livestock.

Instead of competing with wildlife, some people in Kenya have decided to live alongside it and have opened their lands to tourists. This way they can make money from the tourists who come to see the animals. This is called **ecotourism**, and means that both the people and wildlife benefit.

Lions were once hunted as one of Kenya's "Big Five".

A herd of elephants tramples the vegetation near Mount Kilimanjaro in the Amboseli National Park.

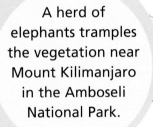

Who benefits?

Tourism does not always benefit local people. In the Masai Mara National Reserve, only two percent of the money goes to local communities. Most of it goes to transport, hotels, and tour companies, many of them foreign owned. Even workers come from other parts of Kenya with 70 percent of them non-Masai.

Conserving wildlife

Back at one of the **safari** lodges in Amboseli, a sign advertises a talk being given by someone from the Amboseli Elephant Research Project. The talk is all about conserving wildlife, so you decide to go along.

Even though Kenya has large national parks, much of Kenya's wildlife is threatened by human activities. Even in the parks, animals such as cheetahs have had their hunting patterns interrupted by the large number of tourist visitors.

Getting to know you

The staff at Amboseli Elephant Research Project know every one of the 600 or so elephants that live there. They identify each elephant by its face, and make detailed notes on their behaviour and friendships.

Mount Kilimanjaro (in Tanzania) towers over the Amboseli National Park, where staff keep a track of all the elephants.

WORD BANK endangered in danger of becoming extinct (gone forever)
illegal against the law

Some animals are so threatened that special action has been taken to protect them. At the bottom of the Rift Valley, Lake Nakuru National Park has an electric fence all the way around it to stop **poachers** from hunting its precious rhinos. The rhino is one of the most **endangered** animals in the world, and Lake Nakuru is a special conservation area set up to protect them.

Ivory poachers are a problem in Tsavo National Park. Armed guards patrol the area to protect the elephant herds, but the park is so large that occasional attacks still happen. At sea, Kenya has marine parks to protect endangered ocean animals such as the dugong, a large seal-like animal.

A special conservation area for endangered rhinos has been set up at Lake Nakuru.

Shop carefully

Wildlife is sometimes killed to make souvenirs for tourists. Shells are collected from the ocean, for example. Crocodile skin can be used to make bags or shoes, and ivory from elephants is used for carvings. These goods are **illegal** to buy, and you should always refuse them if offered.

poacher someone who kills and steals protected animals from the wild

Stay or go?

From Amboseli you catch a local flight to Mombasa and, like most visitors to Kenya, you finish your travels on the beach. The white beaches and warm seas are so relaxing, but there is so much you could still do. The airport is not far away, so if you decide to go home then you are in the right place. But what if you choose to stay?

Lend a hand

Many church groups and charities run projects in Kenya to help improve the lives of people living there. Some take volunteers and provide them with a home and food in return for their help. This is a great way to experience living with a Kenyan family, and lend a hand at the same time.

Still to see and do

If you decided to stay, you could:

- Explore the vast dry lands of northeastern Kenya by taking a camel **safari**.
- Visit with the Samburu or Rendille people and watch a camel race in Maralal.
- Visit one of the large sports stadiums in cities such as Nairobi to see a game of soccer, cricket, or polo.

You could visit the Samburu people and watch the traditional dancing.

WORD BANK dhow type of sail boat

- Sail along the Kenyan coast in a **dhow** to historic Lamu. Located on an island just off the coast, Lamu is one of the last surviving parts of Kenya's Swahili coastal culture.
- Plan a trek up Mount Kenya to the second-highest point in Africa.
- Go fishing on Lake Victoria for a giant Nile Perch – the big ones can weigh more than a human adult!
- Camp in Kakamega Rainforest, the last remaining rainforest in Kenya.
- Visit the Bomas of Kenya in Nairobi to see exhibitions of the many different **ethnic groups** that make up the Kenyan people.

Regional change

Kenya is part of the East Africa region (with neighbouring Tanzania and Uganda). The three countries share their borders and trade goods with each other. They have plans to launch an East African airline and to modernize the railways of the region. They may even one day share a common currency and have a single president.

Locals enjoy fishing off a colourful boat on Lake Victoria.

Find out more

Destination Detectives can find out more about Kenya by using the books and visiting the websites listed below.

World Wide Web

If you want to find out more about Kenya, you can search the Internet using keywords such as these:

- Kenya
- Nairobi
- Masai
- Mombasa

You can also find your own keywords by using headings or words from this book. Try using a search directory such as www.google.co.uk.

The Kenyan Embassy

The Kenyan Embassy in your own country has lots of information about Kenya. You can find out about the different areas, the best times to visit, special events, and all about Kenyan culture.
http://kenya.embassyhomepage.com/

Further reading

Countries of the World: Kenya, Rob Bowden (Evans Brothers, 2002)
Country Studies: Kenya, Heather Blades (Heinemann Library, 2001)
Food and Festivals: A Flavour of Kenya, Wambui Kairi (Hodder Wayland, 2002)
Nations of the World: Kenya (Raintree, 2003)
The Changing Face of Kenya, Rob Bowden (Hodder Wayland, 2002)
World Tour: Kenya, Patrick Daley (Raintree, 2003)

Timeline

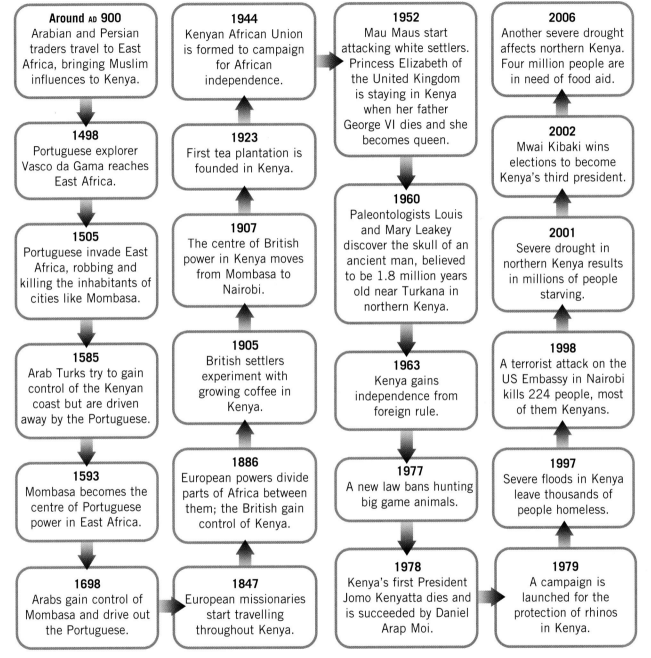

Around AD 900
Arabian and Persian traders travel to East Africa, bringing Muslim influences to Kenya.

1498
Portuguese explorer Vasco da Gama reaches East Africa.

1505
Portuguese invade East Africa, robbing and killing the inhabitants of cities like Mombasa.

1585
Arab Turks try to gain control of the Kenyan coast but are driven away by the Portuguese.

1593
Mombasa becomes the centre of Portuguese power in East Africa.

1698
Arabs gain control of Mombasa and drive out the Portuguese.

1847
European missionaries start travelling throughout Kenya.

1886
European powers divide parts of Africa between them; the British gain control of Kenya.

1905
British settlers experiment with growing coffee in Kenya.

1907
The centre of British power in Kenya moves from Mombasa to Nairobi.

1923
First tea plantation is founded in Kenya.

1944
Kenyan African Union is formed to campaign for African independence.

1952
Mau Maus start attacking white settlers. Princess Elizabeth of the United Kingdom is staying in Kenya when her father George VI dies and she becomes queen.

1960
Paleontologists Louis and Mary Leakey discover the skull of an ancient man, believed to be 1.8 million years old near Turkana in northern Kenya.

1963
Kenya gains independence from foreign rule.

1977
A new law bans hunting big game animals.

1978
Kenya's first President Jomo Kenyatta dies and is succeeded by Daniel Arap Moi.

1979
A campaign is launched for the protection of rhinos in Kenya.

1997
Severe floods in Kenya leave thousands of people homeless.

1998
A terrorist attack on the US Embassy in Nairobi kills 224 people, most of them Kenyans.

2001
Severe drought in northern Kenya results in millions of people starving.

2002
Mwai Kibaki wins elections to become Kenya's third president.

2006
Another severe drought affects northern Kenya. Four million people are in need of food aid.

Kenya – facts & figures

The black stripe on the Kenyan flag represents the African people. The red stripe stands for the struggle for independence. The green represents Kenya's agriculture. The thin white stripes symbolize peace and unity. The warrior's shield covering crossed spears represents Kenya's fight for freedom.

Technology boom

- Internet users: 400,000.
- Telephone lines: 328,400.
- Mobile phones: 1,590,800.
- Internet country code: .ke.

Trade and industry

- Gross domestic product: £20 billion.
- Main exports: tea, fruit and vegetables, coffee, fish.
- Main imports: machinery and transport equipment.

People and places

- Population (2005): 34 million.
- Life expectancy: men – 49 years; women – 47 years.
- Religions: Protestant (45 percent); Catholic (33 percent); indigenous (10 percent); Muslim (10 percent); other (2 percent).
- Highest point: Mount Kenya (5,199 metres/ 17,058 feet).

Glossary

AD time after Christ was born

AIDS epidemic rapid spread of AIDS, a disease caused by a virus transmitted in body fluids. Can be fatal.

algae small plant, similar to seaweed

altitude the distance above sea level used to measure height

ancestor person from whom you are descended

Arabian Peninsula area between Africa and Asia that includes countries like Saudi Arabia

association group of people or organizations

BC stands for "Before Christ"

clan group of families related through marriage

climate average weather conditions of an area

clinic local centre for providing basic healthcare

cooperative group of people working together

coral reef long line of coral, close to the surface of the sea

dhow type of sail boat

diatom small algae-like plant with a shell

ecotourism tourism that benefits local people and does not harm the environment

endangered in danger of becoming extinct (gone forever)

Equator imaginary line round the middle of Earth

escarpment steep slope or cliff, normally on the edge of a valley

ethnic group people who share the same origins and culture

export selling goods to another country

geothermal energy produced by natural heat

habitat environment in which something lives, such as an ocean or desert

healer someone who treats health problems using traditional methods

hide skin of an animal

hydroelectric power generated by moving water

illegal against the law

landslide when a section of land breaks away

mangrove forest type of tropical forest that grows in shallow coastal waters

nomadic people who move around rather than settling in one place

nominee someone suggested for a role or prize

paleontologist scientist who studies fossils to learn about the history of life on Earth

pastoralist someone who lives by caring for livestock

plantain green fruit similar to a banana

plantation large farm growing a single crop

poacher someone who kills and steals protected animals from the wild

population density number of people living in a certain area

provisions supplies of food and other household items

recycled used again for the same or a different use

rural relating to the countryside

safari journey to see wildlife in its natural surroundings.

savannah tropical grassland, often dotted with trees

skewer metal or wooden rod with a sharp end for holding meat whilst cooking

slum area of poor-quality housing

United Nations (UN) global development organization that most countries belong to

urban relating to cities or built-up areas

Index

Akamba 34
Arabian Peninsula 10

British 7, 10, 11, 14
buffalo 38

Chalbi desert 12
cheetahs 40
Cherangani Hills 29, 37
climate 16-17
clothing 35
coast 6, 17, 36, 42
coffee 11
conservation 40-41
currency 6

dancing 34
donkeys 29

education 11, 27
Eldoret 14, 19, 30, 36, 38
elephants 4, 5, 38, 39, 40, 41
ethnic groups 4, 9, 19, 42
export 14, 15

farming 14, 39
fishing 6
flamingos 15
food 24, 32-33
Fort Jesus 10

Gama, Vasco da 10
Government 6, 7, 27, 38

healers 26
healthcare 26
highlands 14, 16, 17

independence 11
Indian Ocean 6, 17
ivory 10, 41

Kabaki, Mwai 11
Karen 21
Kenyatta, Jomo 11

Kericho 7, 15
Kisumu 6, 19, 30
Kitale 14

Lake Naivasha 14
Lake Nakuru 15, 41
Lake Turkana 8, 9, 12
Lake Victoria 6, 15, 43
Lamu 17, 42
landscape 12-17
language 6
Leakey family 8
leopards 38, 39
life expectancy 19
lions 16, 38, 39

Malindi 10
markets 24, 25, 26, 32, 36
Masai 4, 7, 16, 34, 35, 36, 38
Mathare Valley 21
Mathare Youth Sports
    Association 21-23
Mau Mau 10
Mijikenda 34
Moi, Daniel Toroitich
    Arap 11
Mombasa 7, 10, 12, 16, 17,
    18, 19, 30, 36, 42
Mount Elgon 37
Mount Kenya 6, 13, 37, 43
Mount Kilimanjaro 38, 40
music 34

Nairobi 6, 7, 8, 14, 16, 19,
    20, 21, 23, 24, 27, 30, 36
Naivasha 6
Nakuru 14, 15, 19, 30
national parks 4, 5, 16, 36,
    37, 38, 39, 40, 41
Ngong Hills 21
nyama choma 33

Olkaria 14
Olorgesalie 8

pastoralists 4, 12, 24
plantations 14
poachers 41
Pokot 9, 35
population 6, 7, 18, 19, 20
Portuguese 10
presidents 11

railways 7, 16, 30, 31
rhinos 38, 41
Rift Valley 4, 6, 12, 13, 14,
    15, 16, 29, 37, 41
rivers 17

safaris 4, 11, 36, 37, 38, 40,
    42
Samburu 34
savannah 16
seasons 13
slaves 10
slums 20-23, 27
Speke, John Hanning 15

Tanzania 38, 40, 43
tea 7, 11, 15
temperatures 13, 14, 16
tourism 4, 11, 17, 34, 36-39
transport 28-31
trekking 37
Tsavo 16
Tugen Hills 8
Turkana 9

Uganda 7, 30, 43
United Kingdom 11
United Nations 11, 22
universities 27

volcanoes 6, 12, 14

West Pokot 26
wildebeest 16
wildlife 4, 16, 17, 36-41

Titles in the *Destination Detectives* series include:

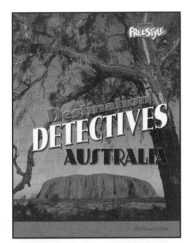

Hardback   1 406 20312 2

Hardback   1 406 20308 4

Hardback   1 406 20306 8

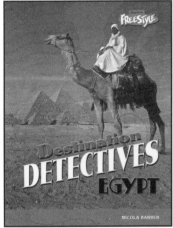

Hardback   1 406 20310 6

Hardback   1 406 20313 0

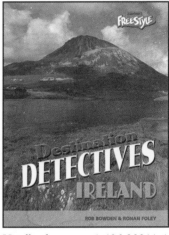

Hardback   1 406 20311 4

Hardback   1 406 20305 X

Hardback   1 406 20307 6

Hardback   1 406 20314 9

Find out about the other titles in this series on our website www.raintreepublishers.co.uk